AMERICA'S 50 STATES

LEARN ABOUT ALL 50 STATES WITH MAPS, FLAGS, AND FUN FACTS!

National Flag

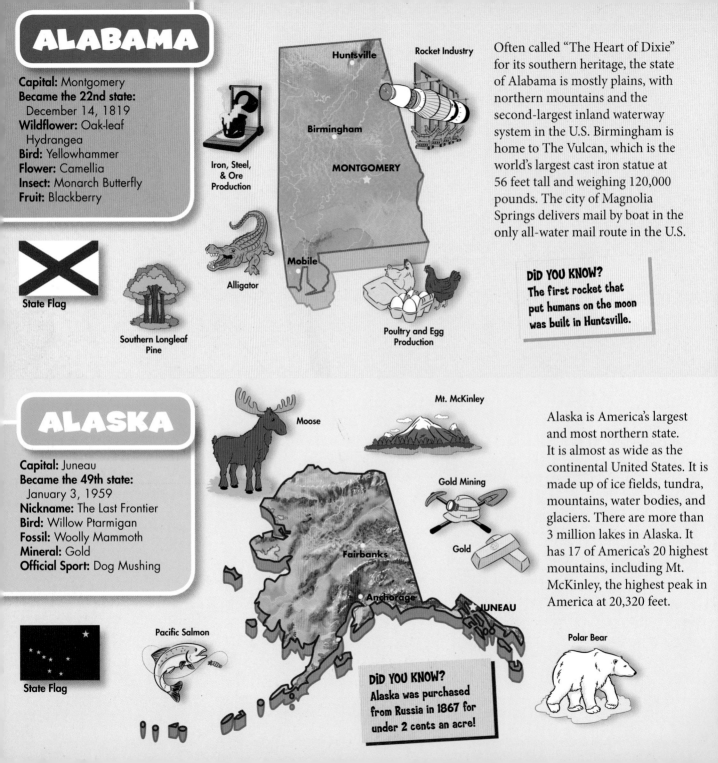

ALABAMA

Capital: Montgomery
Became the 22nd state:
 December 14, 1819
Wildflower: Oak-leaf
 Hydrangea
Bird: Yellowhammer
Flower: Camellia
Insect: Monarch Butterfly
Fruit: Blackberry

State Flag

Southern Longleaf
Pine

Iron, Steel,
& Ore
Production

Alligator

Huntsville

Rocket Industry

Birmingham

MONTGOMERY

Mobile

Poultry and Egg
Production

Often called "The Heart of Dixie" for its southern heritage, the state of Alabama is mostly plains, with northern mountains and the second-largest inland waterway system in the U.S. Birmingham is home to The Vulcan, which is the world's largest cast iron statue at 56 feet tall and weighing 120,000 pounds. The city of Magnolia Springs delivers mail by boat in the only all-water mail route in the U.S.

DID YOU KNOW?
The first rocket that put humans on the moon was built in Huntsville.

ALASKA

Capital: Juneau
Became the 49th state:
 January 3, 1959
Nickname: The Last Frontier
Bird: Willow Ptarmigan
Fossil: Woolly Mammoth
Mineral: Gold
Official Sport: Dog Mushing

State Flag

Moose

Mt. McKinley

Gold Mining

Gold

Fairbanks

Anchorage

JUNEAU

Pacific Salmon

Polar Bear

Alaska is America's largest and most northern state. It is almost as wide as the continental United States. It is made up of ice fields, tundra, mountains, water bodies, and glaciers. There are more than 3 million lakes in Alaska. It has 17 of America's 20 highest mountains, including Mt. McKinley, the highest peak in America at 20,320 feet.

DID YOU KNOW?
Alaska was purchased from Russia in 1867 for under 2 cents an acre!

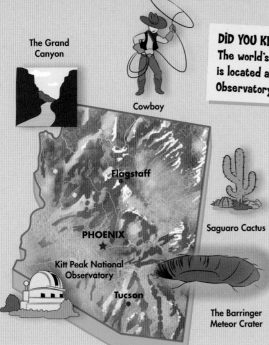

The Grand Canyon

Cowboy

Flagstaff

Saguaro Cactus

PHOENIX

Kitt Peak National Observatory

Tucson

The Barringer Meteor Crater

DID YOU KNOW?
The world's largest solar telescope is located at Kitt Peak National Observatory in the city of Sells.

Arizona is home to many of America's Wild West stories, including the gunfight at the O.K. Corral and battles with Indian chiefs Geronimo and Cochise. Arizona is also home to many of nature's greatest wonders, including the one-mile-deep Grand Canyon, the beautiful colors of the Painted Desert, and the Petrified Forest, where wood has turned to stone! You will also see many different kinds of prickly cactuses in the hot and dry Arizona deserts.

ARIZONA

Capital: Phoenix
Became the 48th state: February 14, 1912
Reptile: Arizona Ridgenose Rattlesnake
Tree: Palo Verde
Gem: Turquoise
Fossil: Petrified Wood
Neckwear: Bola Tie

State Flag

America's only diamond mine is in Arkansas, nicknamed the "Natural State." Any diamonds, amethyst, garnet, jasper, agate, and quartz that you find at the Crater of Diamonds State Park, you can keep! The Ozark Mountains are another natural wonder; they are made of limestone that wears away easily and creates unusual features such as Arkansas' many sinkholes, caves, underground streams, and hot springs.

DID YOU KNOW?
The first fried dill pickles ever sold were made at the Duchess Drive-in in Atkins in 1963.

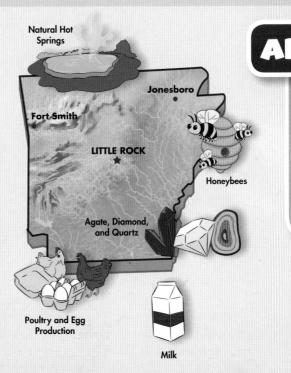

Natural Hot Springs

Jonesboro

Fort Smith

LITTLE ROCK

Honeybees

Agate, Diamond, and Quartz

Poultry and Egg Production

Milk

ARKANSAS

Capital: Little Rock
Became the 25th state: June 15, 1836
Instrument: Fiddle
Insect: Honeybee
Flower: Apple Blossom
Gem: Diamond
Tree: Pine
Fruit: Vine Ripe Pink Tomato
Beverage: Milk

State Flag

CALIFORNIA

Capital: Sacramento
Became the 31st state:
  September 9, 1850
Mammal: Grizzly Bear
Bird: California Valley Quail
Flower: Golden Poppy
Tree: California Redwood
Fossil: Sabre-Tooth Cat
Rock: Serpentine

Avocado Farming

Gold

State Flag

Turkey Production

SACRAMENTO
San Francisco

Death Valley

HOLLYWOOD
Hollywood

Los Angeles

The third largest state, California, was nicknamed the "Golden State" after thousands of people called "forty-niners" went there to find gold in 1849. More people live in California than any other state in the nation. Your favorite actor or actress probably lives in Hollywood, where many movies and TV shows are made. At 282 feet below sea level, Death Valley (in the Mojave Desert) is the lowest and driest point in North America.

DiD YOU KNOW?
Up to 370 feet tall, the world's tallest and oldest trees are in the Redwood Forests. One redwood tree in California is over 2,200 years old. Some trees are big enough to drive through!

COLORADO

Capital: Denver
Became the 38th state:
  August 1, 1876
Animal: Bighorn Sheep
Flower: Rocky Mountain
  Columbine
Tree: Colorado Blue Spruce
Fossil: Stegosaurus
Gemstone: Aquamarine

State Flag

Colorado is known for the great Rocky Mountains that pass through it as part of the Continental Divide (a vast mountain range that runs 3,000 miles from Canada to Mexico). "Colorado" is from a Spanish word for "red" and was named for its red land. The Red Rocks is a large, open-air theater surrounded by giant, red rocks. Colorado has huge cattle farms and many snow-covered mountains for winter sports like skiing.

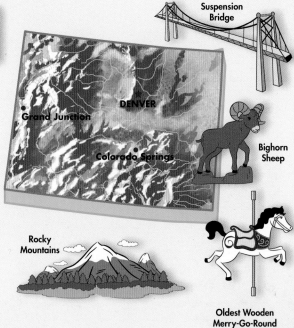

Suspension Bridge

DENVER
Grand Junction
Colorado Springs

Bighorn Sheep

Rocky Mountains

Oldest Wooden Merry-Go-Round in the U.S.

DiD YOU KNOW?
The Royal Gorge is one of the world's highest suspension bridges, at a height of 1,053 feet over the Arkansas River near Cañon City.

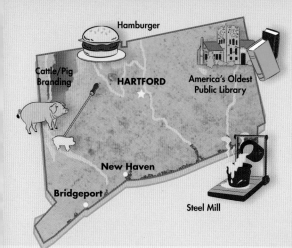

The name Connecticut comes from the Native American word "Quinatucquet," which means "Beside the Long Tidal River." Connecticut is called the "Constitution State" and is one of America's first 13 states. The famous authors Noah Webster and Mark Twain both lived and wrote here.

CONNECTICUT

State Flag

Capital: Hartford
Became the 5th state: January 9, 1788
Nickname: Constitution State
Bird: American Robin
Insect: Praying Mantis
Shellfish: Eastern Oyster
Tree: Charter Oak
Song: "Yankee Doodle"

DELAWARE

Capital: Dover
Became the 1st state: December 7, 1787
Bird: Blue Hen
Wildlife Animal: Grey Fox
Insect: Ladybug
Marine Animal: Horseshoe Crab
Beverage: Milk
Fruit: Strawberry

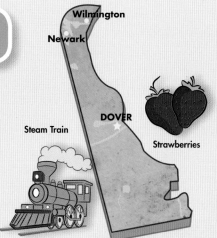

Delaware is called "The First State" because it was the first of the original 13 colonies to accept the U.S. Constitution. It is the second smallest state in America—only nine miles wide at one point! Delaware is known for its chickens, crabs, clams, and manufacturing of chemicals, rubber, and plastics. The Woodburn Mansion, home to the Governor of Delaware, is supposedly haunted by ghosts!

State Flag

Florida, the "Sunshine State," is known for its warm, sunny weather and sandy beaches. It hosts almost 90 million visitors every year. Florida has thousands of islands and lakes. It produces almost half of the world's orange juice supply.

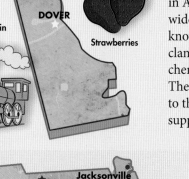

FLORIDA

Capital: Tallahassee
Became the 27th state: March 3, 1845
Reptile: Alligator
Bird: Mockingbird
Animal: Florida Panther
Marine Mammal: Manatee
Saltwater Mammal: Dolphin
Shell: Horse Conch
Beverage: Orange Juice

DID YOU KNOW?
More than 1,000 people move to Florida every day.

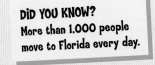

State Flag

GEORGIA

Capital: Atlanta
Became the 4th state:
 January 2, 1788
Amphibian: Green Tree Frog
Butterfly: Tiger Swallowtail
Fish: Largemouth Bass
Fruit: Peach
Insect: Honeybee
Tree: Live Oak

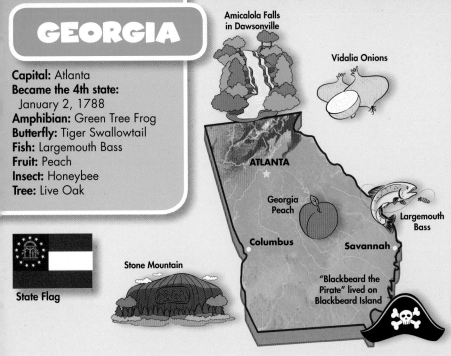

State Flag

Amicalola Falls
in Dawsonville

Vidalia Onions

ATLANTA

Georgia
Peach

Largemouth
Bass

Columbus

Savannah

Stone Mountain

"Blackbeard the
Pirate" lived on
Blackbeard Island

Georgia, the "Peach State," is the last of the
original 13 English colonies. It is known
for peaches, peanuts, pecans, and Vidalia
onions (considered the sweetest in the
world). Historic Saint Marys is the second-
oldest city in the country. During the Civil
War, the fall of Atlanta defeated the South.
The Girl Scouts were founded in Savannah
by Juliette Gordon Low in 1912. Coca-Cola
was invented in Atlanta in 1886.

DID YOU KNOW?
Stone Mountain is one of the largest single
pieces of exposed granite known to the world!
Stonewall Jackson, Jefferson Davis, and Robert
E. Lee are carved on the face of Stone Mountain,
making it the world's largest sculpture.

HAWAII

Capital: Honolulu
Became the 50th state:
 August 21, 1959
Nickname: Aloha State
Bird: Nene (Hawaiian Goose)
Flower: Yellow Hibiscus
Butterfly: Kamehameha
Marine Mammal: Humpback
 Whale

State Flag

DID YOU KNOW?
Hawaii is the only
state in the nation
that grows coffee!

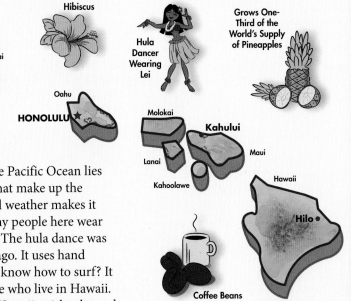

Hibiscus

Hula
Dancer
Wearing
Lei

Grows One-
Third of the
World's Supply
of Pineapples

Kauai

Niihau

Oahu

HONOLULU

Molokai

Kahului

Lanai

Maui

Kahoolawe

Hawaii

Hilo

Coffee Beans

Thousands of miles away in the Pacific Ocean lies
the group of volcanic islands that make up the
state of Hawaii. Its hot, tropical weather makes it
a beautiful vacation place. Many people here wear
flowery necklaces called "leis." The hula dance was
created in Hawaii a long time ago. It uses hand
motions to tell a story. Do you know how to surf? It
is a common activity for people who live in Hawaii.
Early kings and queens in the Hawaiian islands used
to surf on boards in the ocean waters.

IDAHO

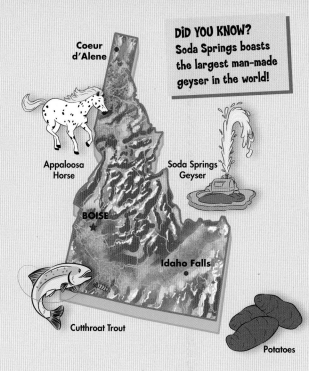

Coeur d'Alene

DID YOU KNOW?
Soda Springs boasts the largest man-made geyser in the world!

Appaloosa Horse

Soda Springs Geyser

BOISE

Idaho Falls

Cutthroat Trout

Potatoes

Idaho is believed to be an Indian name, Ee-dah-hoe "gem of the mountains". Idaho potatoes are known for being the world's best. Idaho grows the most potatoes in the country: 27 billion each year! The deepest river gorge on the North American continent is Hells Canyon. At 7,900 feet deep, it's deeper than the Grand Canyon! A nearly 20-carat diamond was discovered near McCall—one of the biggest ever found in the U.S.! America's longest main street is Island Park's, which is 33 miles from start to end.

Capital: Boise
Became the 43rd state: July 3, 1890
Bird: Mountain Bluebird
Vegetable: Potato
Horse: Appaloosa
Flower: Syringa
Tree: White Pine
Fruit: Wild Huckleberry

State Flag

ILLINOIS

Illinois is known as the "Land of Lincoln" because President Abraham Lincoln spent most of his life there. In 1871, the "Great Chicago Fire" started in a barn, destroying most of Chicago. It took many years to rebuild after this disaster. The first Ferris wheel was displayed at the World's Exposition of 1893 in Chicago. Have you ever eaten at a Dairy Queen? The first one opened in Joliet in 1940. Illinois Senator Barack Obama was elected the first African American U.S. President in 2008.

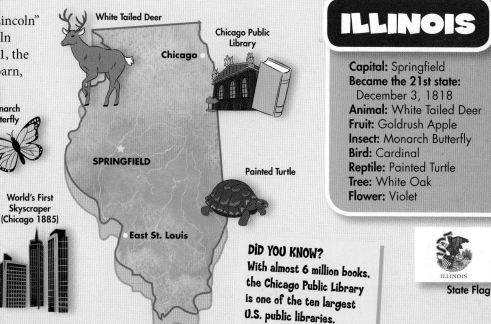

White Tailed Deer

Chicago Public Library

Chicago

Monarch Butterfly

SPRINGFIELD

Painted Turtle

World's First Skyscraper (Chicago 1885)

East St. Louis

DID YOU KNOW?
With almost 6 million books, the Chicago Public Library is one of the ten largest U.S. public libraries.

Capital: Springfield
Became the 21st state: December 3, 1818
Animal: White Tailed Deer
Fruit: Goldrush Apple
Insect: Monarch Butterfly
Bird: Cardinal
Reptile: Painted Turtle
Tree: White Oak
Flower: Violet

ILLINOIS

State Flag

INDIANA

Capital: Indianapolis
Became the 19th state:
 December 11, 1816
Name: "Land of Indians"
Nickname: Hoosier State
Bird: Cardinal
Flower: Peony
Pie: Sugar Cream
Motto: Crossroads of America

State Flag

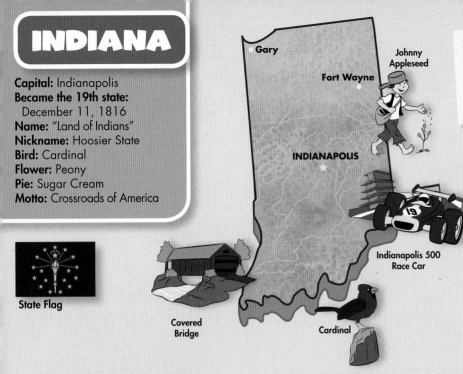

Gary

Johnny
Appleseed

Fort Wayne

INDIANAPOLIS

Indianapolis 500
Race Car

Covered
Bridge

Cardinal

The world's most famous car race is the Indianapolis 500. It is a 500-mile race that takes place every year on a 2.5-mile track. Drivers have to race around the track 200 times! The Speedway is the largest spectator sporting arena in the world. Many people in Indiana gave help and shelter to slaves who used the "Underground Railroad" to become free. Almost half of all Indiana farmland is planted with corn, producing more than 20 percent of the United States' popcorn.

IOWA

Capital: Des Moines
Became the 29th state:
 December 28, 1846
Nickname: Hawkeye State
Flower: Wild Rose
Bird: Eastern Goldfinch
Tree: Oak
Rock: Geode
Song: "Song of Iowa"

The gently rolling landscape of Iowa is where the country changes from forests to grasslands. 90 percent of this land is farmland. Iowa is famous for its corn, soybeans, and hogs. Effigy Mounds National Monument has more than 200 prehistoric mounds built in the shape of mammals, birds, and reptiles. The shortest and steepest railroad in the U.S. is in Dubuque. Herbert Hoover, 31st President, was the first president born west of the Mississippi River.

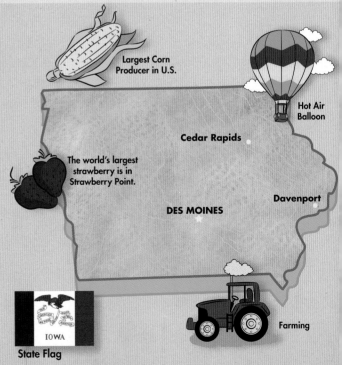

Largest Corn
Producer in U.S.

Hot Air
Balloon

Cedar Rapids

The world's largest
strawberry is in
Strawberry Point.

Davenport

DES MOINES

IOWA

State Flag

Farming

KANSAS

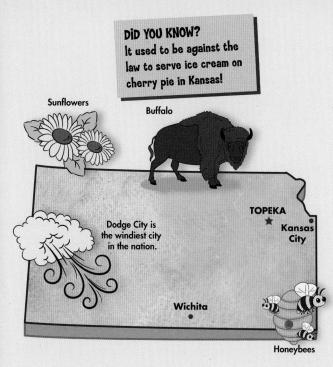

Sunflowers

Buffalo

TOPEKA

Kansas City

Dodge City is the windiest city in the nation.

Wichita

Honeybees

The name Kansas comes from a Native American term that means "people of the south wind." The geographic center of the 48 connected American states is in a Kansas pasture. Kansas is famous for sunflowers, wheat, jazz music, barbecue, tornadoes, and the story "The Wizard of Oz." Kansas City has more barbecue restaurants per person than any other city in the country. Walt Disney's first animation studio was in Kansas City. He fed a small mouse there that he said inspired him to create Mickey Mouse.

Capital: Topeka
Became the 34th state: January 29, 1861
Nickname: Sunflower State
Motto: "To the Stars Through Difficulties"
Animal: American Buffalo
Reptile: Ornate Box Turtle
Tree: Cottonwood

KANSAS State Flag

KENTUCKY

The word Kentucky is from "Ken-tah-ten," or "land of tomorrow." Kentucky is nicknamed the "Bluegrass State" because most of the grass has blue flowers that bloom in the spring. Bluegrass is also the name given to the state's local folk music. Daniel Boone was one of Kentucky's famous explorers. Many settlers followed his trail, "Wilderness Road," to go west. Fort Knox has a big building that holds gold for the U.S. government. Kentucky is known for its coal mines, thoroughbred horse farms, and horse racing. The world's most famous horse race, the Kentucky Derby, has been held at Churchill Downs racetrack in Louisville every May since 1875.

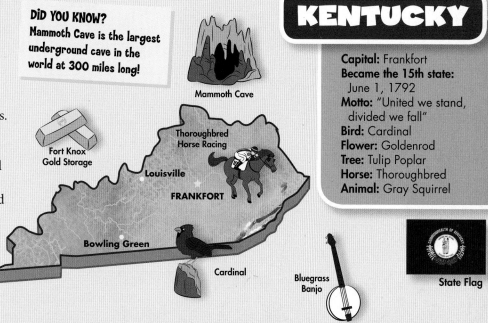

Mammoth Cave

Fort Knox Gold Storage

Thoroughbred Horse Racing

Louisville

FRANKFORT

Bowling Green

Cardinal

Bluegrass Banjo

Capital: Frankfort
Became the 15th state: June 1, 1792
Motto: "United we stand, divided we fall"
Bird: Cardinal
Flower: Goldenrod
Tree: Tulip Poplar
Horse: Thoroughbred
Animal: Gray Squirrel

State Flag

LOUISIANA

Capital: Baton Rouge
Became the 18th state:
  April 30, 1812
Bird: Brown Pelican
Tree: Bald Cypress
Flower: Magnolia
Mammal: Black Bear
Insect: Honeybee
Reptile: Alligator

DID YOU KNOW?
New Orleans is famous for jazz music and the spectacular Mardi Gras festival. with its big parties and parades.

The French settled in Louisiana during the 1700s. In 1803, Thomas Jefferson doubled the size of America by buying the Louisiana Territory from the French. The French influence is still seen in the state's many French names, foods, buildings, and descendants. Do you know what a crayfish is? Crayfish, also called crawfish or crawdads, are small freshwater crustaceans that look like lobsters. Ninety-eight percent of the world's crayfish come from Louisiana!

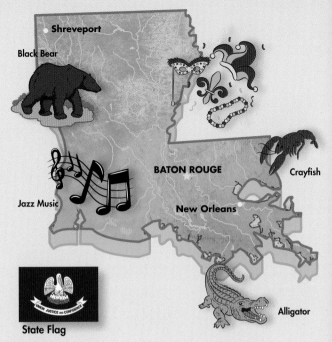

State Flag

MAINE

Capital: Augusta
Became the 23rd state:
  March 15, 1820
Berry: Blueberry
Bird: Chickadee
Cat: Maine Coon Cat
Animal: Moose
Tree: White Pine
Insect: Honeybee

State Flag

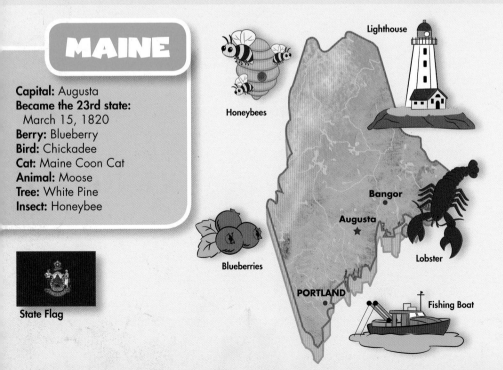

Famous for lobster caught off its rocky Atlantic Ocean shore, Maine is the largest New England state. Nicknamed the "Pine Tree State," 90 percent of it is covered by thick woods. This doesn't leave much room for people, so Maine has the fewest people living here of any other state east of the Mississippi River. Sail Rock is the easternmost point in the U.S. The sun rises here first!

DID YOU KNOW?
The rocky coast of Maine is home to more than 60 lighthouses!

Skiing

Covered Bridge

Mount Washington

CONCORD

Manchester

Nashua

Maple Syrup Producer

State Flag

New Hampshire, known as the "Granite State" for its many granite hills and quarries, is one of the original 13 colonies. New Hampshire was first named North Virginia, then New England, and then finally New Hampshire. Although a small state, it has over 40,000 miles of rivers and streams. The White Mountains take up almost 25 percent of New Hampshire. There, you can see up to 130 miles away on a clear day from the top of 6,288-foot Mount Washington.

Capital: Concord
Became the 9th state:
 June 21, 1788
Motto: "Live Free or Die"
Animal: White Tailed Deer
Flower: Pink Lady's Slipper
Tree: White Birch
Fruit: Pumpkin
Amphibian: Spotted Newt

NEW JERSEY

State Flag

Blueberries

Horse

Newark

Honeybees

TRENTON

Atlantic City Gaming Casinos

Atlantic City

Beach Resorts

Cape May

Capital: Trenton
Became the 3rd state:
 December 18, 1787
Nickname: Garden State
Animal: Horse
Bird: Eastern Goldfinch
Flower: Violet
Insect: Honeybee
Tree: Red Oak
Fruit: Blueberry

One of the original 13 colonies, New Jersey is mostly open land with farms and woods. Most people think of the activities along the Jersey shore's beaches, boardwalks, and amusement parks when they think of New Jersey. Atlantic City and Cape May are popular recreation spots. Many Revolutionary War battles were fought in New Jersey. The 1776 Battle of Trenton was a key American victory in the war.

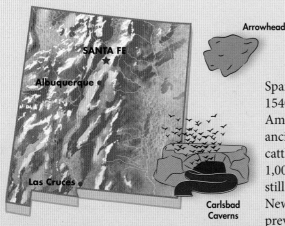

SANTA FE

Albuquerque

Las Cruces

Carlsbad Caverns

Arrowhead

State Flag

Spanish explorers named New Mexico in 1540. This state is known for its Native American history and art, deserts, caves, ancient pueblo dwellings, cowboys, and cattle drives. Taos Pueblo is famous for its 1,000-year-old adobe buildings, where people still live today. An orphaned bear cub from New Mexico was the model for forest fire prevention symbol Smokey the Bear.

NEW MEXICO

Capital: Santa Fe
Became the 47th state:
 January 6, 1912
Nickname: Land of Enchantment
Bird: Greater Roadrunner
Flower: Soaptree Yucca
Insect: Tarantula Hawk Wasp
Vegetable: Chili Pepper
Aircraft: Hot Air Balloon

NEW YORK

Capital: Albany
Became the 11th state:
  July 26, 1788
Animal: Beaver
Bird: Bluebird
Insect: Ladybug
Tree: Sugar Maple
Fruit: Apple
Beverage: Milk

First American Pizza Restaurant 1895

Dairy Farming

ALBANY

First American Chess Tournament 1843

Buffalo

New York City has 722 miles of subway tracks.

New York City

State Flag

DID YOU KNOW?
"The Big Apple" is the nickname for New York City, one of the biggest cities in the world. An old saying in show business was "There are many apples on the tree, but only one Big Apple." New York City is considered one of the best places in the world for fun things to do so it became known as the Big Apple.

From skyscrapers to waterfalls, New York state has it all. Adirondack Park is bigger than Yellowstone, Glacier, Yosemite, and Grand Canyon parks combined. Over 750,000 gallons of water go over Niagara Falls every second. Ellis Island in New York Harbor was where people from other countries who wanted to live in America entered the U.S. The nearby Statue of Liberty is a welcoming symbol of freedom and democracy. It was a friendship gift from France to the U.S.

NORTH CAROLINA

Capital: Raleigh
Became the 12th state:
  November 21, 1789
Carnivorous Plant: Venus Flytrap
Bird: Cardinal
Dog: Plott Hound
Flower: Dogwood
Reptile: Eastern Box Turtle
Mammal: Gray Squirrel

The first English child born in America, Virginia Dare, was born in Roanoke Island, North Carolina in 1587. Do you know the story of Roanoke Island's lost colony? Sometime between 1587 and 1590, a group of English settlers mysteriously vanished. The only clue was the word "Croatoan" carved on a tree. Many think the settlers went to live with the friendly Croatoan Indians, but no one has been able to solve the mystery. The Biltmore Estate in Asheville is America's largest home, with a 255-room chateau and enormous gardens.

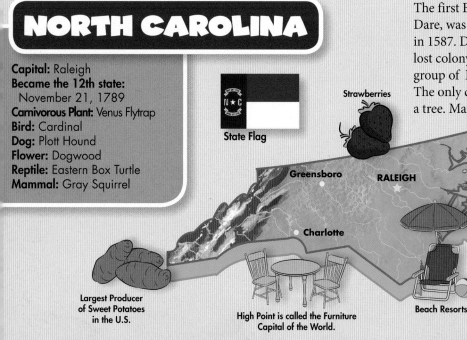

State Flag

Strawberries

Greensboro

RALEIGH

Charlotte

Largest Producer of Sweet Potatoes in the U.S.

High Point is called the Furniture Capital of the World.

Beach Resorts

DID YOU KNOW?
In 1903 at Kitty Hawk beach, the Wright Brothers made the first successful plane flight ever by man!

NORTH DAKOTA

State Flag

Rodeo Cowboy

Soybeans

Stone Obelisk

Milk

Cattle Ranching

Grows more sunflowers than any other state.

Grand Forks

BISMARCK

Fargo

Capital: Bismarck
Became the 39th state: November 2, 1889
Nickname: Rough Rider State
Bird: Western Meadowlark
Flower: Wild Prairie Rose
Tree: American Elm
Fruit: Chokecherry
Beverage: Milk

Not many people live in North Dakota because the northern plains were one of the last areas in the country to be settled. The word "Dakota" means "friend." Historic areas in North Dakota include fur trade posts, military posts, battlefields, trails, and homesteads. Many historic sites in North Dakota are closed to visitors out of respect for Native Americans who hold some of these places sacred. Every other state in America has more trees than North Dakota, which leaves a lot of land for its many grain farms and cattle ranches. North Dakota grows enough soybeans to make 212 billion crayons each year.

OHIO

Between the Ohio River on its southern border and Lake Erie on its northern border, it is no surprise that the name Ohio comes from an Iroquois word that means "great water." For many years no one really lived in northwestern Ohio because it was a wilderness named the Great Black Swamp. Some settlers decided to clear the trees and dig ditches until they drained the swamp, then turned them into Ohio's best farm lands. The Pro Football Hall of Fame is in Canton. Cleveland is home to the Rock and Roll Hall of Fame.

Ladybug

Cleveland

Akron

Canton

America's First Traffic Light 1914

COLUMBUS

The Pro Football Hall of Fame is in Canton.

America's First Hot Dog 1900

Cincinnati

Akron is the Rubber Capital of the World.

State Flag

Capital: Columbus
Became the 17th state: March 1, 1803
Bird: Cardinal
Flower: Red Carnation
Wildflower: White Trillium
Insect: Ladybug
Tree: Buckeye
Fossil: Trilobite
Beverage: Tomato Juice

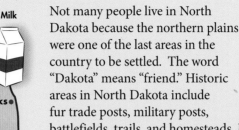
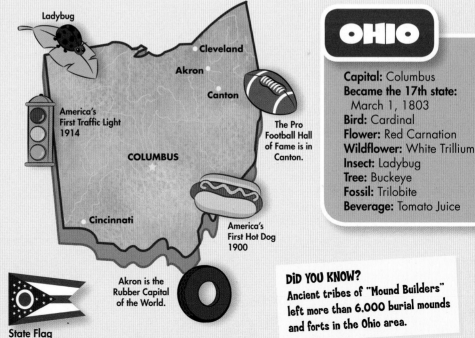

OKLAHOMA

Capital: Oklahoma City
Became the 46th state:
 November 16, 1907
Animal: Buffalo
Furbearer: Raccoon
Bird: Scissor-Tailed Flycatcher
Game Bird: Wild Turkey
Amphibian: Bullfrog
Wildflower: Indian Blanket

Strawberries

Buffalo

Tulsa

OKLAHOMA CITY

Norman

Wild Turkey

White Tailed Deer

Oklahoma is named from two Choctaw Indian words: okla "people" and humma "red". More than 39 Native American Indian tribes and nations live here. Oklahoma grew through oil wells and the sale and settlement of its land. Pioneers lived in early prairie houses called "soddies" that were made from sod (dirt and grass blocks). The last-standing original sod house is now the Sod House Museum. Oklahoma has the most man-made lakes in America (200). More circuses stay in Oklahoma for the winter than anywhere else.

DID YOU KNOW?
The National Cowboy Hall of Fame is located in Oklahoma City!

State Flag

OREGON

Capital: Salem
Became the 33rd state:
 February 14, 1859
Crustacean: Dungeness Crab
Bird: Western Meadowlark
Fruit: Pear
Rock: Thunder-Egg Geode
Tree: Douglas Fir
Nut: Hazelnut

Heceta Head Lighthouse

Snowmobile

DID YOU KNOW?
The world's smallest park, Mill Ends Park, is a circle two feet across, and was created in Portland on St. Patrick's Day for leprechauns and snail races!

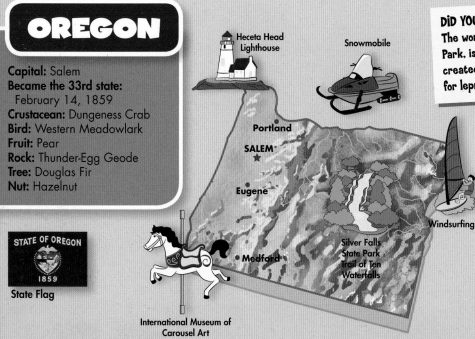

Portland

SALEM

Eugene

Medford

Silver Falls State Park Trail of Ten Waterfalls

Windsurfing

International Museum of Carousel Art

STATE OF OREGON
1859
State Flag

Using covered wagons, many pioneers traveled thousands of miles across America to get to the West Coast using the Oregon Trail. They arrived in a place of amazing natural beauty. Scenic Silver Falls State Park has the highest number of waterfalls in the U.S. At 1,943 feet deep, the crystal blue Crater Lake is the deepest lake in the country. The Columbia River Gorge is considered by many to be the best place in the world for windsurfing. The forested mountains make Oregon a leader in wood products.

PENNSYLVANIA

Full of history, Pennsylvania is one of the original 13 colonies. Philadelphia is home to the Liberty Bell, Constitution Hall, and the first published magazine in America, *American Magazine*. Gettysburg is the site of one of the Civil War's most important battles: the South's final try to invade the North. President Abraham Lincoln also delivered his famous speech here, "The Gettysburg Address," opening with "Four score and seven years ago…" Steel and farming are two of its biggest industries. The Amish are a group of people who live in Pennsylvania without the use of modern technology like electricity.

Capital: Harrisburg
Became the 2nd state: December 12, 1787
Animal: White Tailed Deer
Game Bird: Ruffed Grouse
Dog: Great Dane
Flower: Mountain Laurel
Insect: Firefly
Beverage: Milk

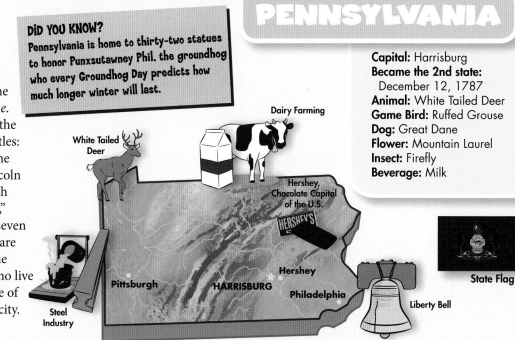

Dairy Farming

White Tailed Deer

Hershey, Chocolate Capital of the U.S.

HERSHEY'S

Pittsburgh

HARRISBURG

Hershey

Philadelphia

Liberty Bell

Steel Industry

State Flag

RHODE ISLAND

The smallest state in the U.S., Rhode Island was the last of the original 13 colonies to become a state. It is nicknamed the "Ocean State" because you can get to the ocean from anywhere in the state in less than an hour's drive. Did you know Rhode Island has the highest proportion of artists of any state in the country? The town of Wickford celebrates these artists by hosting an arts festival every July. What's your favorite kind of art?

Capital: Providence
Became the 13th state: May 29, 1790
Bird: Rhode Island Red
Drink: Coffee Milk
Flower: Violet
Fish: Striped Bass
Tree: Red Maple
Shell: Quahaug

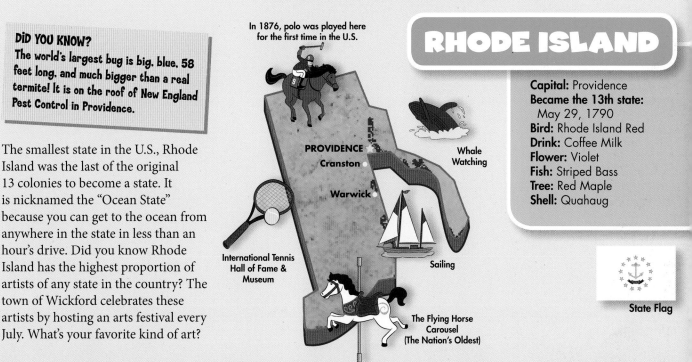

In 1876, polo was played here for the first time in the U.S.

PROVIDENCE
Cranston

Whale Watching

Warwick

International Tennis Hall of Fame & Museum

Sailing

The Flying Horse Carousel (The Nation's Oldest)

State Flag

SOUTH CAROLINA

Capital: Columbia
Became the 8th state:
 May 23, 1788
Hospitality Beverage: Tea
Bird: Carolina Wren
Flower: Yellow Jessamine
Snack: Boiled Peanut
Tree: Palmetto
Fruit: Peach

Famous for southern cooking and growing cotton, South Carolina was one of the original 13 colonies. The first tea farm in the U.S. was created in 1890 near Summerville. The Civil War began in 1861 when the federal Fort Sumter, in the Charleston harbor, was attacked by Confederates. South Carolina has the Palmetto Tree on its flag because this tree helped them during the Revolutionary War. A fort built out of palmetto tree wood absorbed cannonballs fired by the British, so South Carolina won the battle!

State Flag

Gaffney has a water tower shaped like a peach.

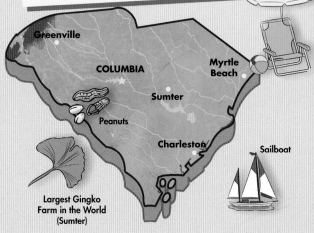

DID YOU KNOW?
Myrtle Beach is a city that lies in the center of the Grand Strand, more than 60 miles of uninterrupted beaches on South Carolina's Atlantic Ocean coast. Myrtle Beach, one of the most popular vacation spots in the country, receives more than 10 million visitors every year!

Greenville

COLUMBIA

Myrtle Beach

Sumter

Peanuts

Charleston

Sailboat

Largest Gingko Farm in the World (Sumter)

SOUTH DAKOTA

Capital: Pierre
Became the 40th state:
 November 2, 1889
Animal: Coyote
Mineral: Rose Quartz
Fish: Walleye
Tree: Black Hills Spruce
Fruit: Blackberry
Sport: Rodeo

South Dakota is well known for Mount Rushmore, a huge sculpture carved into the Black Hills, honoring presidents Washington, Jefferson, Lincoln, and Theodore Roosevelt. Another mountain sculpture, the world's largest, is still being built in the Black Hills. This Crazy Horse Memorial honors the heritage of North American Indians. Bison, or buffalo, used to roam freely in the state but now live in large herds in many state parks for protection from hunting.

Buffalo

Clark is the Potato Capital of South Dakota.

Rose Quartz

PIERRE

Rapid City

Sioux Falls

State Flag

Rodeo Cowboy

The World's only Corn Palace is in Mitchell.

DID YOU KNOW?
If the presidents on Mount Rushmore were real men, they would stand 465 feet tall!

TENNESSEE

Many people visit rock star Elvis Presley's home and gravesite at his estate in Graceland. They also sing a song about Davy Crockett, the famous Tennessee soldier who wore a coonskin cap. Speaking of music, the capital city, Nashville, is known as the home of country music. The name Tennessee comes from the name of a Cherokee Indian village, Tanasi.

DID YOU KNOW?
Reelfoot Lake is known as the "Turtle Capital of the World." It has thousands of stinkpots, sliders, mud, and map turtles.

Great Smoky Mountains

Capital: Nashville
Became the 16th state: June 1, 1796
Gem: Tennessee River Pearls
Bird: Mockingbird
Insect: Ladybug
Tree: Tulip Poplar
Fruit: Tomato
Wild Animal: Raccoon

NASHVILLE
Knoxville

State Flag

Nashville's Grand Ole Opry

Memphis

Tennessee Walking Horse

Ladybug

TEXAS

Bats

Space Industry

Cowboy

Dallas

AUSTIN

San Antonio

Houston

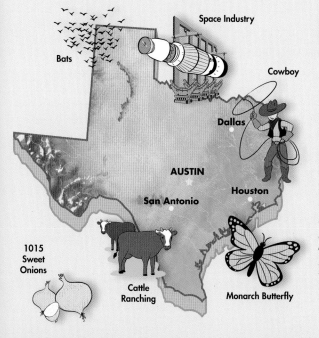

1015 Sweet Onions

Cattle Ranching

Monarch Butterfly

Texas is the second-biggest state in the country behind Alaska. Spain, France, Mexico, and the U.S. Confederacy all owned Texas at some point in its history. In 1836, the Alamo was the site of a famous battle between Mexico and Texas. Texas is famous for oil, natural gas, and cowboys. The Johnson Space Center in Houston is the headquarters for NASA (National Aeronautics and Space Administration). Using space flights, NASA tries to answer questions about space. The name Texas comes from an Indian word for "friends."

Capital: Austin
Became the 28th state: December 29, 1845
Bird: Mockingbird
Flower: Bluebonnet
Insect: Monarch Butterfly
Tree: Pecan
Fruit: Texas Red Grapefruit
Vegetable: 1015 Sweet Onion

DID YOU KNOW?
More species of bats live in Texas than in any other part of the U.S.

State Flag

UTAH

Capital: Salt Lake City
Became the 45th state:
  January 4, 1896
Flower: Sego Lily
Mineral: Copper
Tree: Blue Spruce
Vegetable: Spanish Sweet
  Onion

Utah's name comes from the Ute Indian tribe. Later, Brigham Young led Mormon pilgrims into Great Salt Lake Valley in 1847. The Mormons were "busy as bees" settling in, which gave Utah its nickname, the "Beehive State." The Great Salt Lake is three to five times saltier than the ocean because water does not drain from it. There's so much salt, people float like corks because the salt holds them up in the lake! In the southern desert area are naturally formed wonders like sandstone arches and brilliantly colored spires.

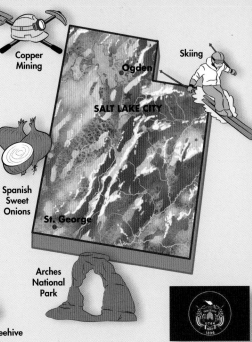

Copper Mining

Skiing

Ogden

SALT LAKE CITY

Spanish Sweet Onions

St. George

Arches National Park

Beehive

State Flag

DiD YOU KNOW?
The average annual snowfall in the Salt Lake City mountains is 500 inches!

VERMONT

Capital: Montpelier
Became the 14th state:
  March 4, 1791
Animal: Morgan Horse
Bird: Hermit Thrush
Flower: Red Clover
Insect: Honeybee
Tree: Sugar Maple
Butterfly: Monarch

Skiing

Largest Producer of Maple Syrup in the U.S.

Burlington

MONTPELIER

Monarch Butterfly

Morgan Horse

Rutland

First Snowflakes Successfully Photographed and Measured 1895

State Flag

DiD YOU KNOW?
The first postage stamp used in the U.S. was made in Brattleboro in 1846!

The name Vermont comes from two French words: vert "green" and mont "mountain." Dairy farming and tourism are Vermont's major industries. Tourists visit Vermont to see leaves turn red, golden, and amber in the fall and to see snow-covered mountains in the winter. Vermont produces more maple syrup than any other state. Being one of the coldest states in the country, Vermont sometimes is too chilly for snow in the winter! The air becomes too cold and cannot hold the moisture that makes snow.

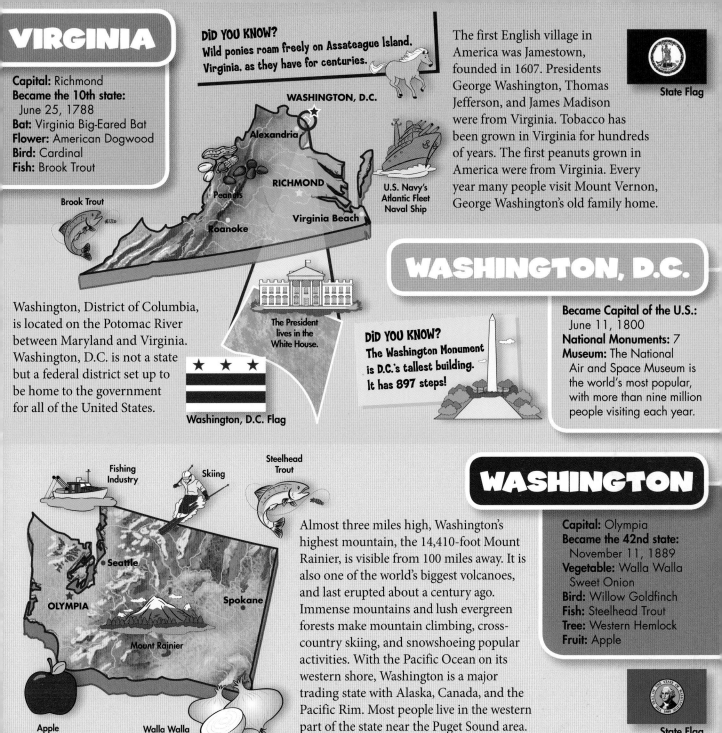

VIRGINIA

Capital: Richmond
Became the 10th state: June 25, 1788
Bat: Virginia Big-Eared Bat
Flower: American Dogwood
Bird: Cardinal
Fish: Brook Trout

DID YOU KNOW? Wild ponies roam freely on Assateague Island, Virginia, as they have for centuries.

The first English village in America was Jamestown, founded in 1607. Presidents George Washington, Thomas Jefferson, and James Madison were from Virginia. Tobacco has been grown in Virginia for hundreds of years. The first peanuts grown in America were from Virginia. Every year many people visit Mount Vernon, George Washington's old family home.

State Flag

WASHINGTON, D.C.

Alexandria

Peanuts

RICHMOND

U.S. Navy's Atlantic Fleet Naval Ship

Virginia Beach

Roanoke

Brook Trout

The President lives in the White House.

Washington, District of Columbia, is located on the Potomac River between Maryland and Virginia. Washington, D.C. is not a state but a federal district set up to be home to the government for all of the United States.

Washington, D.C. Flag

DID YOU KNOW? The Washington Monument is D.C.'s tallest building. It has 897 steps!

WASHINGTON, D.C.

Became Capital of the U.S.: June 11, 1800
National Monuments: 7
Museum: The National Air and Space Museum is the world's most popular, with more than nine million people visiting each year.

Fishing Industry

Skiing

Steelhead Trout

WASHINGTON

Almost three miles high, Washington's highest mountain, the 14,410-foot Mount Rainier, is visible from 100 miles away. It is also one of the world's biggest volcanoes, and last erupted about a century ago. Immense mountains and lush evergreen forests make mountain climbing, cross-country skiing, and snowshoeing popular activities. With the Pacific Ocean on its western shore, Washington is a major trading state with Alaska, Canada, and the Pacific Rim. Most people live in the western part of the state near the Puget Sound area.

Capital: Olympia
Became the 42nd state: November 11, 1889
Vegetable: Walla Walla Sweet Onion
Bird: Willow Goldfinch
Fish: Steelhead Trout
Tree: Western Hemlock
Fruit: Apple

Seattle

OLYMPIA

Spokane

Mount Rainier

Apple

Walla Walla Sweet Onions

State Flag

WEST VIRGINIA

Capital: Charleston
Became the 35th state:
 June 20, 1863
Animal: Black Bear
Bird: Cardinal
Flower: Big Laurel
Tree: Sugar Maple
Fruit: Golden Delicious Apple
Butterfly: Monarch

Seneca State Forest
Morgantown
Black Bear
Cardinal
CHARLESTON
Huntington
Monarch Butterfly
Brook Trout

DiD YOU KNOW?
Nearly 75 percent of West Virginia is covered by forest!

State Flag

West Virginia is nicknamed the "Mountain State." The average altitude is 1,500 feet above sea level, making it the highest state east of the Mississippi River. West Virginia used to be a part of Virginia before it became its own state. The coal mining industry is an important part of West Virginia's history.

Wisconsin is called "America's Dairyland" because it is a top producer of milk, cheese, and butter. In fact, some Wisconsin residents wear funny hats that look like cheese and call themselves "cheeseheads." People from all over the country visit the famous Wisconsin Dells, tall sandstone cliffs and unique rock formations on the Wisconsin River formed by melting glaciers. Milwaukee is home to Harley-Davidson, the most famous motorcycle company in the world. Harley motorcycles are nicknamed "hogs."

WISCONSIN
1848
State Flag

Eagle River: Snowmobile Capital of the World
Bloomer
Green Bay
MADISON
Milwaukee
Dairy Farming
Corn

WISCONSIN

Capital: Madison
Became the 30th state:
 May 29, 1848
Rock: Red Granite
Animal: Badger
Bird: Robin
Flower: Wood Violet
Tree: Sugar Maple
Grain: Corn

WYOMING

Capital: Cheyenne
Became the 44th state:
 July 10, 1890
Flower: Indian Paintbrush
Mammal: Buffalo
Bird: Meadowlark
Reptile: Horned Toad
Tree: Plains Cottonwood
Sport: Rodeo

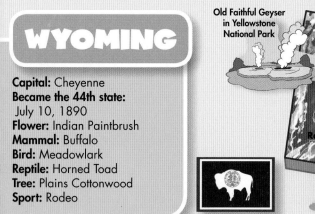

Old Faithful Geyser in Yellowstone National Park
Coal Mining
Casper
Rock Springs
CHEYENNE
State Flag
Buffalo

Millions of visitors come to the first national park, Yellowstone, each year. It is home to more geysers than any other place on Earth, including Old Faithful, which erupts on a predictable schedule. Wyoming has vast plains in the east and mountains in the west. Wyoming has the lowest population of any U.S. state. Wyoming was the first state to give women the right to vote and to elect a female governor.